Mamiaith
Ness Owen

ARACHNE PRESS

First published in UK 2019 by Arachne Press Limited
100 Grierson Road, London SE23 1NX
www.arachnepress.com
© Ness Owen 2019
ISBN: 978-1-909208-77-3

Thanks to Muireann Grealy for her proofing.
Printed on wood-free paper in the UK by TJ International,
Padstow.

Acknowledgements

Willows and *Mowing* published in Fat Damsel Journal October 2016

March published in Culture Matters Journal February 2017

Traed Berffro published in Poetry Wales Spring 2012

Stand Your Ground published as *A Potion to Leave the Past Behind* in Ink, Sweat & Tears May 2016

Mamiaith (English) published in *Responses to poems by RS Thomas* RS Thomas Festival 2018

Mr Naoto Kan Vists published in Red Poets 2016

One Name – Cymru published in Red Poets 2017

Email published in Here and There: the life of a global citizen 2017

Lobsgows published in MsLexia 2018

Female Blackbird Sings published in *Dusk,* Arachne Press 2018

Ei Chân (Yr Aderyn Du) published in Rhaw (A literary journal) Many thanks to Iona Evans for helping with this translation into Welsh

Yr Apêl oddi wrth Ferched Cymru (1923-24) was exhibited for the 80th birthday of the Temple of Peace, Cardiff

Many thanks to Sian Northey for fine tuning and proofing Ness's translations of *Mamiaith, Un Enw, Hogan Lan Môr.*

https://waleslitexchange.org/en/authors/view/sian-northey

Ness says: Many thanks to editor Cherry Potts for taking this collection on, and being very patient.

Mamiaith

Contents

Willows

He planted one for each
of us and one for her we
lost whose name we only
whispered to the sea-wind
determined for life they
grew each season, roots
entangled branches spread
spindling away from each
other until I forgot which
one was me but she was
immortal in the garden where
we played in upturned-wardrobes
and buried broken promises
through the window I blew her
goodnight kisses as November
winds tore leaves from her branches
and I watched her wave goodbye
knowing spring would bring her back.

.

Mowing

I try to follow my
father's straight lines
like he taught me
but he moves in spirals
Sometimes a job just
needs to be finished
doesn't matter how.
We take it in turns
it's easier to follow
his tracks though
I do cut corners
and change direction
just to prove I can.
Turning in spirals
makes me dizzy and
it hurts to cut
daisies, dandelions
plantain, buttercups.
He knows I'd love
to keep them but
if we don't keep on
top of this, we know
it'll outgrow us.

March
21/1/17

They wanted us broken
stranded away from our-
selves and each other rifts
deepening between us
drip-fed fear, anger, hate
it's always someone else's fault
they wanted silence no-one
to question why difference is
a problem, a worry, a threat
silence won't shape our future
end hate-driven discontent
watch us gathering, hear
the tread of our feet like
others before us marching
for what we know is right
our voices not alone but
amplified louder than
the ballot-box, join us
march where you're standing
they can't ignore us all.

Traed 'Berffro*

Not as bad as Auntie Annie's feet
which pointed west, toes plaited
that kept you staring long
after it was polite to stop
but definitely traed 'Berffro.
No denying it
she'd been squeezed into
the wrong shoes.
The Chinese they used to
bandage girls' feet you know
to keep them small
The Welsh they go to chapel
The ache of ill-fitting
hand-me-downs
is like the ache of saying no
and the pull to the west
in my one pair of well-worn shoes.

*Aberffraw Feet

Zero

*'a type of punctuation
mark so that all numbers
are kept in their correct place'*

Zero-hours
there is no obligation
Zero rights
you're, as you know you are,
Zero respect
a most-valued member of staff
Zero protection
your reputation is regarded
Zero commitment
so highly here with us
Zero credit
we've many hours for you
Zero time off
during term time of course
Zero control
the thing is there's no money
Zero power
cuts have to come to us all
Zero tolerance
time to gather our stories
together voices will be heard.

The Meeting

Never could sit still
clock watching
legs swinging
last question p-l-e-a-s-e
life is outside this room
beyond retention
attainment, completion
imagine all the somebodies
somewhere starting their
own quiet revolutions
leading their own rabble-
rousing masses onto
unmarked paths with
no arrow telling them
which way to go
make a decision
(*Yes, I know it's hard*)
but choice is yours
you can sit and fester
watch scales of anger
burst through your skin
or the door is open
can you still walk?

Stand your Ground

Take
yoga breaths, pins, pressure points
camomile, beta-blockers, Diazepam
fill the void with Jesus, Mars Bars and vodka
fill it with l-o-v-e, hate and oxygen.

(Sing)
You can't turn back
Only walk forward

Blink
trust your instincts
run!

Catch a fleeting moment
*dal dy dir**
stay in

forgive everyone
give up, give in
let go

and write and
write and dance
and write and dance.

Repeat

*stand your ground

15

Laboon*

Listen to us, immersed in water
who swim before we walk
breath the rhythm of tides
live the smallest footprint
in our world there is no take
no want, no mine
our stories will save us.

Listen for the absence of bird call
the silenced wind
see the smooth retreating ocean
the sand struck boats
the wave is hungry again.

Old stories tell us
run for mountains
row for deep water
sea spirits warned of
my girl already green
with a belly full of sea
told elders run with her
over their shoulders
to bring back her breath.

This is our universe
If there is no one
to tell our stories
how will we prepare?
This is Laboon.

*Laboon or 'The wave that eats people' is a name for tsunami in the language of the nomadic Moken people of Thailand. They all survived the 2004 tsunami because of their stories.

Mamiaith

Pwy wnaeth ddwyn y geiriau
o geg fy mam a'u taflu yn
ôl ataf mewn darnau sy'n
disgyn i'w lle yn fy mhen ond
yn gwrthod disgyn ar bapur?
Fel perthynas annisgwyl, yn dal
ag ogla capal, yn twt-twtio yn
fy nghlust, ysgwyd ei phen
a thrio fy neud yn ddiarth i fy
eitifeddiaeth.
Wyrion y 'Not' pryd nawn ni
dorri'r cortyn? Sut nawn ni
ddweud ein stori yn yr iaith fain?
Yn baglu ac ymddiheuro
dan ni'n anadlu Mamiaith
yn barod am chwyldro
ond yn gwybod y bydd ein
hysgrifen yn ein bradychu.

Mamiaith*

Stolen from my mother's
mouth, thrown back to me
in pieces that fit so neatly
inside my head but will
not fall onto the page.
Like an *un*invited relation
still smelling of chapel
she tuts in my ear, shakes
her head, tries to make
me a stranger to what's
already mine.
Grandchildren of the Not
When will we break the chord?
How do we tell our story in
a thin language? Tongue-tied
excusing our way through
we breathe in Mamiaith
waiting to be unearthed
always knowing our
pen will betray us.

*Mother tongue

Hogan Lan Môr

Ganwyd rhwng dau fôr
croen dŵr hallt, yn
droednoeth ar y tywod
mae'n cyffwrdd adra.
Y llanw sy'n gwthio
a'i thynnu yn ôl, ar goll
yn gwybod does dim
byd yn ei dal fel y môr.
Mae wastad yn gwybod
bod o'n disgwyl amdani,
hitha a'r rhai â ddewiswyd
y mamau sy'n gadael drysau
heb eu cloi i blant neith byth
ddod adra.

Hogan Lan Môr
(Seaside Girl)

Born between two seas
with salt-water tasting skin
barefoot on sand
she touches home.
Currents push and pull
her back lost and sick
with knowing, nothing
will hold her like the sea.
She knows it's waiting
for her with the other
chosen few whose
mothers leave doors
unlocked for children
that are never coming
home.

Un Enw

Mae'n dechrau gydag
enw nid cyfieithiad
sut fedran ni fod yn
estron yn ein gwlad ein
hunain? Bobl y werin
rhwng heli'r môr a
chysgod mynyddoedd
yn brwydro yn erbyn
pob camddehongliad
i gadw ein hiaith;
iaith y nefoedd.
Wedi ein creithio gan
gestyll, cloddio,
boddi ond heb
ein tawelu, yn dod
o hyd i'n llais ein
hunain i adennill,
gair ar y tro, dim ond
un enw sydd ei angen.

One Name – Cymru

I read once that to be born Indigenous is to be born an activist – just the state of being and existing is a form of resistance to oppression

Dawn Dumont

It starts with a name
not a translation
someone tell me when
did we become foreign?
We are *pobl y werin**
shouldered by sea
sheltered by mountain
standing up to each
misinterpretation
to keep our precious
language of heaven
castled, mined, drowned
but not yet silenced
finding a voice that
is ours to reclaim
a word at a time we
need only one name.

*People of the land

Yr Apêl oddi wrth Ferched Cymru (1923-24)

Mae'r dyfodol yn llawn
gobaith ar hyd y llwybrau
a fo orau gennych, felly y
cychwynnwyd, yn eich
amser da eich hunain.
Hiraethwn am y diwrnod
pan na throir at y cleddyf
cerdded braich ym mraich
gan garu pawb yn gadarn.
Heddwch drwy gydymdrech
heddwch i fyd cyfan.

The Appeal From the Women of Wales (1923-24)

The future is full of
hope along the fairest
paths you possess, this
is how it begins in your
own good time. Long
for the day when there's
no turning to weapons,
walk arm in arm, truly
loving everyone.
Peace through solidarity
peace to the whole world.

This was written using the words in the peace petition
The Appeal to the Women of the United States of America 1923 – 1924
which was signed by 390296 women (60% of the women in Wales)

Ei Chân
(Yr Aderyn Du)

Mae dy gân yn dawelach
na'i gân o, wedi d'eni
yn gwybod y bydd rhaid
i ti drio'n galetach ond
'rwyt yn dal i ganu
nid yn unig â dy wddf ond
adennydd a chynffon yn
taflu dy lais â nerth fel
petaet yn boddi yn y
byrdwn hyd nes i ti
ddal yr union nodyn
i lonyddu pob dim.
Ym mrig y nôs newidir
trefn y byrdwn,
daw'r olaf yn gyntaf
gyda nerth yn yr annisgwyl,
nid oes neb yn d'adnabod
ond o'r diwedd
maent yn gwrando.

Female Blackbird Sings

Your song isn't
as loud as his
born knowing you'll
have to try harder
still you sing not
just with throat but
wings and tail forcing
out your voice like
you're drowning in
the chorus till you
find the one note
to stop them still.
At dusk the order
of chorus reverses
last becomes first
power lies in the
unexpected
they don't recognise
you but at last you
have their ear.

Lobsgows*

Nain is boiling the bones of
some unfortunate creature
on tip-toes I peer into
the shineless pot
blue and smooth they
bob up and down like
they're fighting for their
last chance of escape
She says I'm as deep as
the ocean when I ask
what animal they're from
lifts my chin with warm
crooked fingers
there are some things
we don't need to know
at the window I watch
steam drops falling
stopping some half-
way like I'm their god
she quietens me in a
language of side-glances
with onions, carrots,
rwdan** she silences the pot.

*Traditional Welsh stew
**swede

Email

A oes posib cael y neges yn yr iaith Gymraeg?*

Just another email
amongst the many
spat into the inbox
why would it matter?
Translation costs and
*un*fortunately there
aren't any Welsh-speaking
assessors (at the moment)
but the option to take
training in the language
of your choice was of
course always offered
but after all in seven and a
half years *no*body had
taken the opportunity
to sit in the far corner
of the classroom with
translated pages around
their neck slowly tightening.

*Is it possible to have the message in Welsh?

Watching Her Leave

Car wheels spiral
slowly unravelling
the years between us
smile frozen
womb-aching
hands counting
all the waves I can
fit before she's gone.
Roads of goodbyes
stretch before me
first days for her.
Sensing the slack
my wild-heart beats
louder than the
voice wishing her
back to the breast
and I know this is
right, this is the
order of time. The
earth breathes out
as my feet reground
my fingers uncurl
and she lets me go.

Counting

After A

There are twenty-four steps
to his office, two plus
four makes not enough
I'll have to find another.
He says we're all normal
in our own way and who
wants to be normal anyway
diagnosis is not an exact
science it's a process of
elimination, he could find
Greek or Latin names for
me but they won't make
me better, labels (he says)
make life easier for every-
one else and there are four
pencils on his desk and a
Biro, four plus one is safe
there are five palms trees
in the photo he took
in Sri Lanka, (he says)
I really must go there
one day, if I get the chance.

Ta'im o dan draed neb*

I spend my days
trying to find you
or the part of you
I know I'll never
understand
I almost catch you
on corners, arriving
too late I study your
language read your faces
understand your pride
is as hard as the granite
we live on, layered with
silent misunderstandings
never wanting to be
under anyone else's feet

*Literally *I will not be under anybody else's feet*

Shut Up

Been telling me
shut up all my life
stand up straight
keep your nose clean
and your mouth shut
think what you want as-long-as
it don't come out your gob
shut my mam up with pills
my dad with bacco and lush
call this living? Nothing changes
same shit, just another year
corruption everywhere, all
around me, all these people
that's supposed to be good
nobody's listening so I got
to get louder, start shouting,
someone's got to throw the
first stone. You know I'm up
for it 'cos everyone'll blame
me, I looks the part, don't I?
a suitable psycho, fit for the
job, smoke's like this wall
you can't get round it
flames higher than me
reaching out raging
I hear them shouting
you can't ignore me
I'm here I'm in your
face and I burn.

Mr Naoto Kan Vists

(*A Warning from Fukushima*)

Whilst most of us in the Chamber did not agree
with what Mr Kan had to say...
Our support for nuclear power does not come at any cost...

Honesty is his name
regret in any language
looks much the same
he talks of his semi-circle turn
of technology incompatible with life
behind Wylfa-Shima signs
gaunt steel giants watch
the sky breathes starlings
the road of opportunity throbs
draining young blood from our island heart.

RE: Mud

*Plans to dredge 300,000 tonnes of mud from near a disused nuclear
plant and dump it off Cardiff Bay have been criticised.*

(*Why?*)
A simple question. Pause
for the age-old answer we
don't need to remember,
it sleeps on our tongues,
grows old with our bones.
(*It's because they can.*)
Couldn't we find words, our
mother-tongue has so many.
Didn't she teach us how to say no?
Time tells us choose your battles,
ebb-tides are longer than floods
but how do we argue with
half-lives of billions, fourteen days
notice or jobs at any cost?

#10 Ways to Say No (to radioactive mud) Without Using the Word 'No'
(FAO EDF, Y Senedd, Natural Resources Wales etc, etc)

1. Agree
Sure, bud. As soon as we're back in Europe, we'll have your mud.

2. Offer an alternative
How about you put it somewhere else instead?

3. Distract
Look at our football team and we're not even afraid to fail…

4. Write an IOU for it
Let me write an IOU. You can claim it after we have our independence.

5. Remind her of prior infraction
Remember last time you….(choose from list)

6. Sing it
The N says Nnn… the O says oh… Every letter makes a sound and together they make….

7. Appeal to the logical part of her
Common sense and some basic information can greatly
reduce radiation exposure and risk for most people i.e. by
not taking contaminated mud.

8. Look it up
I don't think you can dump radioactive mud, cariad.
Let's look it up.

9. If you can't beat them, join them!
I know! We need to get rid of some mud too. Where
shall we put it?

10. Use a (bilingual) sign
And the sign says, Dim diolch.*

*(No thanks)

Wild Geese

I open the window to autumn
heard them shooting since dawn
low-flying in the morning rain
echo, their unmistakable sound.
Each down-beat of wing, slow
and measured, keeping each
other in line and they've been
shooting all morning but there's
no distress call only silenced
raised heads ripple through
the flock and I'm close enough
to hear their wings rustle to
join them in their fall from life
circling and letting go and I'd
heard the shots all morning
but sometimes you just forget
don't you?

Digging

Digging your garden
are we looking for
answers in feather,
shell, slate, bone,
fragments of your
life earth-scented
dropped, lost, broken
layers of moments
connecting us
passed from hand to
hand, things we leave
behind, buried truths
telling part of our story
the one we couldn't shout.

Pebble Collector

In my pocket
washed-up, sea-worn
wasted on the non-
believer who doesn't
see time etched on
the surface or hear
the breaking of the
seventh wave
traces of us,
another time
when skin was
supple, bones
were softer
one of a million
on that beach
on that one day
unremarkable as
the moon's pull
of the tide.

Disgwylfa Chapel

It took five office days
from the first slate taken
in the September sun by
fluorescented men swarming
at an open wound that let the
light pour in and a silent chorus out

Deffrwch* Ebenezer,
Hebron, Salem, Elim,
Tabernacl, Hyfrydle,
Bethel, Noddfa

free from an arched embrace
a skeleton of youthful rafters
to a thousand unholy
shades of grey.

*Wake up

41

Kiss
(Dancefloor Dignity)

He said he was a botanist
in his best Cofi* accent like
I wouldn't know what it meant
his lips are cold and he presses
too hard but he looks like
Sonny Crockett in his pastel
rolled up sleeves
least I kissed a bird tonight
he slurs into my ear
my eyes open wider
he doesn't look like Sonny
Blue Stratos stings my nose
I don't like being called a bird
drowning in dry ice
swimming in Blue Moons
I slap him with my
white patent handbag
and walk away in my
matching patent shoes
I don't look back.

*Caernarfon

Buzzard

There is something
reassuring in her cry
like a mother calling
endlessly searching for
the dead, still hunting
a scent wakes her into
flight
wingspan stretched
she bares her colours
soaring skyward
perfectly powerless
to a mob of ravens
who would force
her to the ground
she circles higher
catching thermals
riding ridge lifts
remembering always
to drift with the wind.

Dwynwen

Is there a heavier
weight to carry
than a burden
that isn't yours
when your soul
cries to love what
your heart allows?
In dreams I asked the
universe for a chance
of a quiet life no egg-
shell stepping, side-
glancing, heart-bursting
day after day fight
isn't it enough to
think for myself
and no-body else?
She started replacing
my questions with a
wasp-waisted content
unfinished my wounds
drained the music from
my bones and finally
she cured me of love.

Blodeuedd

Impatient flower
waiting to bloom
no one is born a woman
no one should remember
birth into a world of rules
no mother's milk to soothe,
to tell of your place in the
world, to share stories
of your people in a warm
language without words
uncertain as spring you
grew towards the light
awakened by the waxing
crescent moon. What will
they do with a flower-woman
who's tasted choice?
What will they do?

Boys of Summer

Jesus is dead. Not
the Jesus, but *our* Jesus
long-haired and sandalled
he lies in the dunes, clutching
the beer barrel like his one
true love.
That's what you get (*they* tell us)
when you've more money than
sense and a mother who orders
whiskey to the door.
So this is death his half smile tells
us. The marram grass whips and
the salt wind kisses, *in the blink
of an eye* he takes a breath.

No-one is Watching

The tired tick of
the unwatched clock
shakes the cobwebs
fools the spider that
supper is near and
the first snowflake falls
tickling Moel Faban's*
side. Temperatures rise
they say before snow
but not inside the van.
Cocooned in layers you
drift into the silver-grey
abyss before sleep and
dream of another life,
before needles and lies.
No-one is watching
sleep washes away the
pain of wanting. The
mountain's deaf to the
deepening of your breath
as cold tightens her grip.

*A mountain in North Wales

How to Begin

Begin with fearlessness
eyes open wide bathing
in the warm newness
of the undiscovered
uncoiling the spiralling
desire to taste, touch, see
with uncomplicated senses
to dance an inner smile
barefoot on home soil
slowly soaking in the
inevitable joy of being.